Disturbing the Dust

Peggy Seely

Clare Songbirds Publishing House Poetry Series
ISBN 978-1-947653-92-4
Clare Songbirds Publishing House
Disturbing the Dust © 2020 Peggy Seely

Printed in the United States of America
FIRST EDITION

Clare Songbirds Publishing House was established to provide a print forum for the creation of limited edition, fine art from poets and writers, both established and emerging. We strive to reignite and continue a tradition of quality, accessible literary arts to the national and international community of writers, and readers. Chapbook manuscripts are carefully chosen for their ability to propel the expansion of art and ideas in literary form. We provide an accessible way to promote the art of words in order to resonate with, and impact, readers not yet familiar with the siren song of poets and writers. Clare Songbirds Publishing House espouses a singular cultural development where poetry creates community and becomes commonplace in public places.

140 Cottage Street
Auburn, New York 13021
www.claresongbirdspub.com

Contents

How Dare You Imply That My Mother
                Was Not a Strong Woman   7

There Came a Day   8

Throw Away the Key   9

Bill of Goods   10

Letter to the Me I Used to Be   11

Thank Your Lucky Stars   12

Parkland   13

Disturbing the Dust   14

Just as the Sun is about to Set   15

How to be Upper Crust   16

Top Drawer   17

Reflecting   18

Something About Time   20

That Music, This Memory   21

Green Soap   23

I Want to Talk with My Sister Today   24

Changing Direction   25

Repair Shop   26

A Matter of Perception   27

Out of the Darkroom   28

Set Aside   29

The Interview   30

What I Can Never Write About   31

The Book Fair   32

Thank God for the Lawrence Welk Show   33

I Walked with a Confident Strut Back Then   34

That One Evening   35

Lusting in My Heart Like Jimmy Carter   36

Lanais are for Hiding   37

Seminar for Lunch   38

Best Laid Plans   39

Underlying it All   41

Acknowledgments:

Bill of Goods appeared in Wrestling the Ghosts (Foothills Publishing 2016)

Thank you to Clare Songbirds Publishing House, the Editors and staff who made this book possible.

Thank you to The Poetry Workshop in The Villages, Florida and The Writers' Group in Canastota, NY.

Special thanks to my friends, loyal fans, and loving, supportive family.

I remain grateful for lovers of poetry and those willing to be persuaded.

Photograph of the author courtesy of Donna Ward

Dedicated to strong women the world over

How Dare You Imply That My Mother
Was Not A Strong Woman

Pundits, positioned for the cameras
Trending. Fashionable
Current hairstyles
Current blather
These are women. Discussing women
Judging women
Women who have been abused
Victimized women
who, these self-styled authority figures proclaim
are weak
How dare you! How dare you imply that my mother
was not a strong woman!
My mother is the immigrant girl riding a streetcar
to a convent. The boy she births is a bastard abandoned
by the bastard she scrubbed floors for. My mother
is the waitress in an all-night diner, shift ending in time
to ready her children for school, cook the dinner
he will fling against the wall because of his bad day at work.
My mother is a farmer's wife, racing a storm to save crops
in the field, absorbing his wrath because she "failed".
Weak, declare the Talking Heads, because these women are poor,
uneducated, *they somehow deserve it* hangs in rarefied air.
How dare you.

My mother is a teacher married to a raging football star
who signs autographs for police
and they leave her alone with him.
My mother graces a penthouse, campaigns, raises funds,
nurses her bruises when the music dies and the bottles lay empty.
My mother is every woman
who stays to protect her children
who lies to protect his reputation
who challenges the culture that creates her
who believes
who persists
who rises
who lives
Do not say our mothers were not strong women!

There Came a Day

Fish-fry day, Manager leered,
made a big show of sniffing,
said, "Good Morning, Girls!"

Exam day, Professor
handed the freshman her test,
"I can make sure you pass this."

Performance review day, HR Director
checked off a few boxes,
"There's an easier way for you to advance."

Game day, Coach and Team
shared their fantasies with the cheerleaders,
"Oh, that's just locker-room talk."

Rehearsal day, Producer
invited the understudy to his office,
"You can be the star of this show."

For a while these "girls" simply smiled
because *Boys will be boys, Oh it's harmless,
Ignore it.* But there came a day
"Enough. Enough. Enoughenoughenough"

Then, Manager   Professor   Director
Coach   Team   Producer
Doctor   Lawyer   Pilot
Preacher   President
said, "We should have been watching their eyes."

Throw Away the Key

That door was barred, closed for good, I thought.
Then along came Kavanaugh. Discourse. Hostility. Vitriol.
I thought of my sons: the professor is especially vulnerable.
The minister could easily be accused. Falsely.
The accounts manager in an office where women dress provocatively.
Well, don't they? Some of them.
When Dr. Christine Ford spoke, I wept.
And my door burst open.

Why this time? Similar events through the years didn't cause that.
But she told of the room where it happened, who it was.
No doubt, no doubt at all.
So many details she couldn't recall so she is of course lying.
So many details escape me too. What part of the year it was.
Who else was in the house. Was there a party? Noise
on the other side of the door? I know I was ten.
I know who it was. I see the bed. My bed where I used to be safe.
I feel his breath on my neck. I know where his fingers are.
He had come to my house often. He said he wouldn't be able to again
if I told anyone. I liked him to come. He brought presents,
sang funny songs.

I didn't tell anyone. He did come to the house again.
I wouldn't look at him. I left the presents untouched on the table.
We moved away by the time I turned eleven, when I closed that door.
For good, I thought. Then along came Kavanaugh.

Bill of Goods

*The feminine mystique has succeeded in burying millions of American
women alive. The only way for a woman ... to find herself, to know
herself as a person, is by creative work of her own. There is no other
way.* ~*Betty Freidan*

Like most little girls back then
I was force-fed fairy tales—
someday my prince would come;
or a knight in shining armor.
I had to be pretty, though; Cinderella,
not the ugly step-sister;
industrious like Snow White,
singing while I cleaned up after
a bunch of grumpy dopes.
I could even lay like death,
looking lovely of course, and a single kiss
from some guy passing by
would make truths out of all my dreams.
Ads in my mother's ten-cent
movie magazine promised eternal bliss
if only I used the right douche so HE
wouldn't turn away in disgust. What's
douche, Mom? Give me that!! Go play!
So I grew up smiling, sweeping,
swooning and sniffing. And stifling.
Princes came and princes went.
Then one day my shining knight did appear.
In the form of an un-princess-like book-writing
woman.
The Feminine Mystique exposed!

Now what shall I do?
Abjure my penis envy? Refute the label
neurotic and stand on my own dainty feet?
Love my children even as I leave them,
bringing back lessons from the outside world?
What a concept! First stop—book store.
I need to replace everything on my shelf.

Letter to the Me I Used to Be

Hey Blondie, braids unraveled
hanging from monkey bars
by your skinny skinned knees
Someday when they're made of metal
you'll set off sirens at airport gates
Bounce around more before it's too late

Flirty Miss Teen, sashaying down the street
daring one special boy to see
Once you unlock your secret vault....
(no need to read between the lines)
I'm telling you straight
Wait

Let that sailor-boy ride his ship to glory
His shouldn't be your story
Stay in school headstrong fool
You'll earn a scholarship easy
Study Shakespeare, study law
Design self-driving cars
Be the first female astronaut on Mars

Keep stars in your eyes a little bit longer
Someday you may be a wife, a mother
You'll find it's great,
but let the mortgage the grocer
the orthodontist the PTA wait

Well you didn't listen so here we are
twilight of life and I'm taking stock
There were plenty of chances
to make "better" choices
but that's a judgment call

and I didn't try to have it all
Do his arms cradling me still
on disquieting nights beat a view
of a framed PhD from a virginal bed—
In being as honest with you as I can
Can I honestly say: No regrets?

Thank Your Lucky Stars

I hung out with a group of church ladies
and learned to say blessed instead of lucky.
Blessed as in I didn't die giving birth
like my momma did. Blessed as in
my man came back from Vietnam
and still had a leg. As in twelve weeks
of chemo might shrink my little girl's tumor.
Blessed the fire skipped the barn;
but today on Facebook I saw this:
Every atom in your body came from a star that exploded.

Well.

It said I wouldn't be here if stars hadn't exploded.
It said all the things that matter
(speaking of evolution)
were created in the nuclear furnaces of stars.
Carbon, nitrogen, oxygen, calcium.
Phosphorus.
The stuff I'm made of. It didn't say a word
about some naked guy's rib, one he had
no use for in the first place, apparently.
Yeah, that's good for my self-esteem.
What else it said was *So, forget Jesus.*
Stars died
so that I could be here today.

I can just hear the church ladies.

Parkland
February 14, 2018

What a disservice I've done,
dismissing them as shallow, self-absorbed,
heads buried in iPhones.

Today I watch them, hear them, feel their fear,
smell the spilled blood. Their passion is contagious.
They are color-blind. Self-labeled *Privileged,* they reach
across miles, across cultures to their opposites.
My suppressed hope unfurls like seedlings in spring.
All day I see, I weep, I bleed.

I sleep, dreaming of a world united.
I have lived with teen-agers. Loud, demanding,
contentious, simmering teen-agers

who don't back down. Who won't give up
and I stand with students who will stand free
of cynicism, of hate, safe in a world of their own making.

Disturbing the Dust

I dreaded going into Aunt Mollie's house.
A Great Horned Owl with piercing yellow eyes
glared as I opened the door.
Of course he was stuffed and they were glass
but that didn't keep them from following me
as I sidled warily past the table it perched on
coughing from the dust Aunt Mollie didn't see anymore.

Worse, Uncle Fred of the dragging leg and thumping cane
shared the shabby place; floors groaned, windows moaned,
things unknown scuttled in the walls.
Most punishing though, inside Aunt Mollie's house,
was the smell. Like being wrapped in wet wool.
Like worn-out shoes forgotten in the corner.
Hair, maybe, that needed washing; old people.

That was it! Old people!
The smell in my Grandmother's room as I visited.
When I was grown with children of my own
my father came to stay. It clung to his flannel shirts,
the ancient Army cap he refused to throw away.
Now, my beloved and I? Old people. Every morning
I fluff his pillow. His aroma wafts upward and saves me.

Just as the Sun is about to Set

July twilight at Bow Lake
grandsons calling "boat ride!"
and she'd leave dishes half done
                          stride to the dock
apron-drying her hands
not expecting the setting sun to wait.

I sat with her once on porch steps
the cracked Mexico bowl filled with strawberries
between us
a storm simmered to the west
She pinched off hulls slow and exact
pronounced us too young to marry
                        I, and her son.
I pulled away sharp when our fingers touched.

In her college yearbook 1918 it says
she will be an author in New York
marry the class poet, not fall unplanned into love
                        bear seven babies, serve potato soup.

She'd planted lilacs in her Victory Garden
brought some to me when my son was born.
Please put them in a vase, I'd said, not reaching.
I'm so clumsy with my hands, she'd say
but every one of us has a hand-knit heirloom
                        to toss across a sofa.

Is Grandma staying a month this time?
In the bus station a man tried to rob her.
She stopped her visits; it was our turn to travel.
How patiently she out-waited our excuses.

I expect her to be writing.
                        It always annoyed me
the hours she spent
jiggling the table with her words. I have them all
somewhere. She isn't writing. Her pen rests
capped, on the bedside table.
                        I take her hand.
It lies in mine like a November leaf.

How to be Upper Crust

I didn't like my mother-in-law
nor she, me
I was much too young
when I married her son
and I didn't come with a pedigree

My people got here in steerage
hers on the Mayflower
She reminded me of it in small ways
I let that give her power

She held my babies on her lap
She held Joni's in her heart
She let me know in small ways
I didn't let her know it hurt

She got her degree from the Ivy League
I didn't finish high school
She mentioned it in small ways
I let myself feel a fool

At the table I watched her
butter her bread
in aristocratic bits
So that's the way I do it
now
when I dine in fine circles
I silently thank her for showing me how

Top Drawer

Who would think a dresser drawer could hold a man?
I open it and there's my dad.
He'd walk a mile for a Camel. *I inhale deeply when he lights up.*
Pungent smoke rings fill the air. Afterward, he chews Sen-Sen,
offers me some. I had learned the secret of the package:
slide the little box from its cardboard sleeve, shake tiny squares
from a hidden hole to mask your tell-tale breath.
Sharp licorice/anise flavor made me shudder. *Yes, thank-you*
because he was my hero and I refused him nothing.

I find a faded photo: on a bicycle, he wears dress pants,
shirt collar loosened under a stylish tie, blond hair thick,
mustache that tickles when he kisses my cheek. *I am three,*
perched on the handlebars, clinging for dear life,
clad, like he usually is, in overalls; ribbons in my braids,
lacy-cuffed socks in boy-like shoes. I don't remember
having a bracelet but here it is. My expression, captured in sepia,
suggests, *I hope this fellow knows what he's doing.* Or is it that
this dapper being is unfamiliar, newly back from wherever he goes?

Under a stack of tattered hankies (now you can buy them
 "Vintage Farmer's Handkerchiefs" on eBay for double-digit prices)
is the mouth organ he carried on The SS Lapland in 1922
from Germany: Hohner 12 Chromatic Harmonica. Key of C.
Strains of Red River Valley, Aura Lea float from the rocker
on the porch. Sheltered under the pear tree, I cradle my rag doll.
Mom is baking cinnamon rolls. I can hardly wait!
The box I have labeled "Dad" holds everything. Almost everything.
Closing the drawer on innocence, I summon the Goodwill driver.

Reflecting

In her later years, my mother-in-law shared a discovery:
"As I stroll the avenue, I glimpse a reflection
in a department store window and I think,
Now who is that old lady? and then I realize it is I!"
Yes, she spoke that way. She'd raised seven children
with the help of her English teacher's salary
when language was respected, full sentences expected.

How would she navigate 2019? If only she'd exposed enough
of herself for me to predict! Back then, I conquered avenues,
stilettos tapping, red tresses tossing—(from a bottle but who
knew)? Aging was a four-letter word. Then
I married her son and learned to tone it down a little
My sons are the long-hair short-words variety
Congrats, they say. Why waste three syllables?

She kept a line-a-day diary since high school. I happened
upon it open on her desk one day. You would've peeked too
Pinochle with the Abbots; they the winners, was one line
Cooked chicken for Sunday's pot pie was another
Made lesson plans for the week. Returned library books
Picked beans, bought cracked eggs from Tuttles
Daddy home early. She referred to her husband that way.

Each day noted high and low temperatures. One entry
that stayed with me read: Home from hospital with Baby 5
name undecided, letter from Aunt Betty, baked gingerbread. I'd
been told how she taught school the day she gave birth, first
four no clue they were about to get a new sibling. In town, at
school, she was a saint, more so when Daddy was arrested one
night, released in the morning. No line on that day.

Never a line for a feeling. Expectation. Joy. Anger. Regret.
To her mother she was a spendthrift, wasted $2 on curtains
for her dorm room. To her Professor, a disappointment, didn't
become an editor or marry the class poet. To her offspring, a
role model: do the right thing, don't question, don't complain,
don't cry. To her grand-children she was a ready partner for
card games, a reader of countless stories.

I admired her, felt threatened by her, yearned to be her, disliked
her. She complimented my hair. Chastised me for a late thank-
you note Watched my kids so I could visit my sister. Once I
invited her to lunch, ordered a lobster roll; she requested a cup
of hot water, added catsup, ate it with a spoon.
Knitted an afghan in my favorite colors.
Rewrapped and returned a Christmas gift I'd sent her.

President of the Board of Education, she awarded her son his
diploma and shook his hand like any other student.
A member of the D.A.R. Church.
Her suits were severe, prematurely white hair in a tight bun. But
I saw her on her knees in the dirt, wearing a faded house-dress,
rescuing a bird. The time I confided in her an unforgiveable act
by my husband, her son, she advised me:
Treat him like Cary Grant.

Today, when I stroll the avenue, catch my reflection, say with a
start *Now who is that old lady* I think of her.
I was never able to answer her question. And, I believe,
neither was she.

Something About Time

Test like this for Alzheimer's they told me.
Draw a clock-face, have her put the numbers in.

I'll choose the moment. It's a little game, I'll say.
Like counting the tulips. Remember?

Sixteen, she'll say. Like my candles.
The year I had my first cigarette.
You didn't know that, did you? She is triumphant.

Yes, I did. Yes, I do. Oh lord, how I do.
This conversation isn't new.

Did you bring me one? Anticipation flares.
Joy lights her face. The shake of my head destroys her.

We talk about the clock. She doesn't want to do it.
I make her take the pen. It's just numbers, Mom, I say.
Like when you helped me with arithmetic. Remember?

She holds the pen at arm's length. Uncurls her fingers.
It smacks the floor. Again, triumphant.

All right, I sigh. I have to go home now.
Her eyes empty. I'll try to come tomorrow.

My hands are shaking too much to get the key right.
I sink to the steps and stare at the future.
All the clocks in my house are digital.

That Music, This Memory

Cartoon of a guy so skinny he slipped through a straw,
we dubbed him Frankie Snotrag
Jitter-bugged in the gym to Chattanooga Choo Choo,
hungered for dinner in a diner
Pushed the tips of our noses up to mimic Dick Haymes
crooning You'll Never Know, giggled because he never would.
Doing chores to Boogie Woogie Bugle Boy, *Decca* in gold
on a blue label, The Song Spinners
Comin' in on a Wing and a Prayer, One motor gone,
they still carry on.

I searched the weekly list of our boys missing or dead,
prayed with my cousin her boyfriend's name wasn't on it,
patted her shoulder while she sat on the grass and cried.
My dime allowances, quarters my loving aunt taped to my
birthday cards, saved. Not for records, we had no player.
Paper dolls! Even The Mills Brothers were gonna
buy themselves one. I chose Betty Grable
because I planned to be her when I grew up,
Deanna Durbin because I couldn't carry a tune.

Music poured from the Philco, transforming our working-class
living room. Till the End of Time drifted through its mesh;
people surged into streets shouting The War is Over!
Fireworks, horns, hugs, bedlam.
August 1945 two months before I turned ten.

A shadowy memory from those years: standing on the porch
of a house on a street under a lamp post, a woman beside me.
Wearing coats. I had mittens on.
Was she my mother? A suitcase. A woman in the barely opened
door with light behind her. You'd Be So Nice
To Come Home To melted from the lips of Dinah Shore.

A half century passes. My mother and I ride in a car.
She is faded, frail, mind still sharp.
We notice a vintage diner, stop for pie and coffee.
I Had the Craziest Dream Last Night confesses a
young Frank Sinatra from a jukebox.

Oh, mom says, I know that song, the years when you were lit-
tle. I ask her, Did you and I ever stand on a porch, it was cold?
Dark. A suitcase. A woman opened the door.
Oh that, Mom says. She was your father's new girlfriend.
I packed your clothes. I told her You want him?
Here. Take his kid too.

Green Soap

Search aisles, find face cleansers, body wash, liquids
galore, everything but a good old-fashioned bar
of soap. The kind secured in wrapping that shivers
you with a paper cut if you open impatiently,
maybe sealed in shiny foil, or slipped into a small
cardboard box. Whatever I open, scent escapes like
Genie from a bottle and bathes me in memories.

I'm at Aunt Anna's about to take a bath after helping
in her garden all day. She has it ready; we wait outside
the door while Uncle Tony goes in with his ruler to
measure two inches of water in the tub, not a drop more.
It costs money for water, more money to heat it. Uncle
Tony comes home from the coal mine needing to soak in
water up to his chest before he shows himself at supper.

Just now, I peeled paper from a thick rectangle of gold
whose spicy fragrance wafted me to Aunt Josie's bedroom.
She kept bars of soap in closets, dressers, to chase moths away
she said. The weeks I was too sick for school, but mom had
to work, Aunt Josie piled pillows behind my head, fed me
broth and ice cream from silver spoons, read me away to places
filled with color, kissed my forehead, left a soft light glowing.

When Mom let Pop back into our lives, he moved us to
a farm with no electricity, no running water. Laundry day
was daunting, pump water outside, carry buckets inside
to heat on the wood stove, scrub clothes bending over a
washboard. Green soap in a bottle stung like wasps when
poured on scrapes or poison ivy; wasn't meant for cleaning.

Soap for washing clothes had a memorable use the
day I came home from the library with a new word.
A friend had put her thumb over the B on a book
titled *My Dog Buck*. Change B to F, she said
collapsing in giggles. In my eight-year-old innocence
I asked my Mom that evening what it meant.
That's when I found out what Fels Naptha tastes like.

I want to talk with my sister today

She'll drive an hour, I'll drive an hour; we'll cheek-kiss hello at a mall
We'll sigh for pretty dresses at least two sizes too small
Vow to lose twenty pounds before the next time we meet
Stop for coffee, order fries and fudge sundaes to eat
We'll mention weather, traffic, breaking news, and then
Make a disparaging comment or two, in general, about men
Which leads to a discussion of how husbands can disappoint
Complaints re: our kids. *You'll never guess who I caught with a joint*!
We'll reflect on our childhoods—far from the best
She'll remind me that I was a terrible pest
We'll disagree on the memories we share
That rattlesnake Pop killed on the porch; we found it there
No, he stretched it along the running board of our old car
I taught you Chopsticks. *No, you taught me Twinkle Little Star*
All of a sudden it's five o'clock; we'll get giddy on a glass of wine
Over-tip the waiter for taking too much of his time
We'll have cried a little, laughed a lot, said Let's not wait so long.
I couldn't know then how hard it is now that all our tomorrows
are gone

Changing Direction

Near the car window a face appeared
dark against the dark
I couldn't let him see me check the lock
He tapped on the glass. *You lost?*
I wouldn't admit it
Instead I told him the place I was looking for
Follow me and as I did, I said to myself
"Am I stupid?"
He climbed on the bike I hadn't noticed
motioned me to drive along
led me to a crossroad, pointed
flashed a thumbs-up, pedaled away

Repair Shop

He looked like Rosey Grier
Not that I'm big on football but Rosey
was big in the news then, also from Georgia
Front office girl called me in
New hire for the Parts Department
Welcome, Willie. I put out my hand
A black mountain of a man, head bent
hands stayed at his sides. He didn't look up

Ma'am, he answered mornings to my greetings
Sat alone with his lunch bucket
while the mechanics clustered at my desk
Did crap jobs he was given, on time
no complaints, mumbled replies
never lifted his head to any woman
Once I had to squeeze past as he changed tires
Put my hand lightly on his back

How could a man so big whirl so fast!
Fist shot up with a tire iron, eyes blazed
mix of fear and fury. My own went wide
I backed into a stack of boxes. Oh god, Willie
sorry. I didn't mean—I'm sorry. Easing, he
became the Willie I knew. Thought I knew.
1960s. Georgia. What had he seen? Been through?
I kept my distance. This was no gentle giant

In Brooklyn I'd taken for granted black classmates
I couldn't identify what I felt about Willie
Not fear. Not pity. Just a longing for him to look up
Six months or so, it happened. Our eyes met
for a split second; he said Hi. Friday he took
his check straight from the payroll clerk's hand

A few more weeks, he dropped the Misses and Ma'ams
Came to our picnic and played softball. Soon after
joined our lunch group. We cheered when he told us
he had a girlfriend. Gettin' married, he said, y'all come

It's 2020 today and sometimes I think about Willie
big like Rosey, head down.
And the way I saw him that day, grinning
as we toasted his future.
Because everything is different now.
Isn't it?

A Matter of Perception

She was blonde
She was buxom
She was boisterous
"Pain? Honey, you ain't known pain
'til your man run off
with a skinny-bitch flirt
from the Sam's Club."

She wiped the counter where my frothy drink
had left a puddle and leaned over.
Avoiding her cleavage
I met her eyes. She winked.
"I see the books you been readin'."

First it was *Divorce and Its Aftermath*
Then I brought *Adjusting to the Single Life*
Today it's *How to Survive in a Man's World*

"I could write one a them," she said with conviction.
How ta Feed a Passle a Kids on Minimum Wage.
"You got kids, honey?" She patted my naked left hand.
"Louse even took the ring back, huh?
You'll be okay. You'll make it. I tell my girls:
Be careful out there. Lovin' don't last. Pain do."

My smile was tentative.
I didn't know what to say to her.
I slipped a twenty under the plate
retrieved my book
went back to the university library
to study harder for the BA in psychology
I'm this close to earning.

Out of the Darkroom

I am an old photograph
in an old-fashioned photograph book,
cornered, shoved into tiny triangles,
stuck in place. Edges blurred. Faded.
I am memory. I am reminiscence.
Someone will turn a page and there
I'll be. Neither black nor white. Not
in living color certainly. Sepia, maybe.
I like to say it. Seep eee ah. Defined:
brown pigment from ink-like secretion of cuttlefish
Good grief! Well, yes, on reflection,
from a secretion.
Now look up cuttlefish. Like "cuddle."
Pleasant images: babies, puppies, fleecy blankets
on frosty nights. Instead...*10-armed mollusk
differing from related squid*...eeewww.
Not a pleasant image. Not a pleasant word even.
I don't care to be related to a squid.
(Too many years I had need of ten arms, though
Eyes in the back of my head, too)
...having a calcified internal shell...
Now we're getting somewhere.
From the Gr. sepein: to make rotten.
Is that it, then? I am an old photograph.
Sepia.

Set Aside

The old man blocks half the produce
painstakingly picking through grapes
in plastic bags. I shop other aisles, return.
Still he bends to his task
ignoring carts tangled in the small space.
Finally, huffing, I squeeze around him
noticing only then he works here, his job:
tidy up the merchandise on display.
I grab a container of raspberries.
These have fuzzy ones, I mutter, replacing it.
Give it here, he grumps. Don't put it back
if there's bad ones in it.
I thrust it at him. Here, I snarl in return.
It's not my job to find them.
Glancing over my shoulder
before I dash away, late to home and dinner,
what I see is a little boy, eyes lively
fingers nimble. Is he thinking, When I grow up
I want to be an old man in a supermarket
sorting through bags of sweet grapes
culling the few gone rotten.

The Interview

She loves to do interviews, she tells me
lays out a pad, 3 yellow wooden pencils
very sharp
pierces her cigarette stubs
into a tiny Vesuvius of shreds
Nobody accuses me of high tech!
she's proud of that.
You look good, d'ya like my hair?
new young boyfriend, new young cut.
she fluffs it. *Too red, d'ya think?*
hair dresser called it "cherry pop"
She gives a slow wink. *Expect me to resist that?*
can ya tell no bra? my guy doesn't like 'em too perky
'member when Katie Couric was perky?
Hey look! skinny jeans! my son-in-law
whistled. *It's the body right not the years.*
She curls one shoulder forward
barks out a laugh. *Did ya hear your neighbor*
down the street got picked up
for shoplifting? Cops hushed it up, tho'.
I happen to know one of 'em. Her hubby
cheats on her. Guess she's acting out.
So your kid made Dean's List, huh?
That's what passes for news in this one-horse town!
The Baker kid, one built like a Greek god, y'know?
Dumber 'n' a box o' rocks. Not gonna graduate.
I happen to know a guy on the school board.
Kid's mom'll freak. She's already seeing a shrink,
did ya know? I did that once, can you believe it?
My ex pushed for it. Damn shrink said I was
superficial! Me! I ooze love and, what'd'ya call it?
Empathy! I adopted, betcha didn't know that.
Insisted on another race. I dig all colors.
Listen, come over to my pool sometime.
Work is slow on this ten-cent weekly local.
The bark again. She strikes a match.
Ya don't mind, right? Inhales with gusto.
This is such a garbage job. These people.
Not you, I don't mean. You're okay.
Ready to tell me about your smart kid?
I really do love doing interviews.
She frames her chewed eraser in a smile.
Lay it on me, honey, she invites.
Your secrets are safe with me.

What I Can Never Write About

In the Creative Writing class I registered for
when Interior Decorating filled early
the question: What can you never write about?
Centipedes wriggled to mind.
Then, on paper, I turned over a stone.

Snakes. But one summer my new power mower
decimated a nest of them—fodder for a poem.
Shakespeare because I never studied him
not having stayed in school long enough
but I answered a prompt with a parody, earned an A.

Love-making (fantasy too scintillating not to print).
Let's see. Things too painful. Suicide.
My nephew shot his way into my memoir.
Of course I can't write about
man's inhumanity to man

although I started researching the Holocaust
after my visit with Aunt Gussie.
So my answer is, definitively, gossip.
Now let's sit down over a nice cup of tea
and chat.

At the Book Fair

A woman rushes to my table
whips my book from her satchel
slaps it down in front of me
orders "sign this!"
With a look of triumph
she shoves it back in her pack.

A pudgy man in a cowboy hat
picks up my book, says he'll
journey tomorrow to New Jersey
to be a donor for his sister's
stem cell transplant, needs
something light to read.

I say This isn't it.
Nodding, he touches
two fingers lightly
to the brim of his hat, walks away.
Arms linked, an elderly couple
move like snails

past each eager author
showing not the slightest interest.
Dodging between tables
a small boy waves aloft
a big sticky lollypop. Where
was the gate-keeper.

Striding by in a black leather jacket
is a fierce-looking man with tattoos
covering a hand big enough
to nearly hide a book of poetry.
Just as an obnoxious loud-speaker
demands *clean up, clear out*

a woman regal in her wheelchair
reads of my love for native hills
where I hiked relentlessly in my youth
return each summer to climb again.
She buys my book, looks me straight
in the eyes, and without a word, moves on.

Thank God for The Lawrence Welk Show

Bombarded by breaking news, daily news, fake news,
real news, all the news that's fit to print, or not,
I am angry, sad, frustrated, bewildered, exhausted.
Inundated with ads infinitum, warnings, scandals,
protests, vitriol, pathos, violence, scams,
I am exhausted, bewildered, frustrated, sad, angry.

I sit on the couch at the end of a day, bowl of popcorn
without butter, glass of something green that looks
and tastes like I imagine cud must,
but guarantees I will live to 100,
and I say why in this world would I want to? To watch
my grand-children grow and prosper? But what of bad guys
with guns? Cancer-causing water, if they even have water?

What of hacking, and fracking, and tracking their every
move by someone, something, out there, intent on evil?
What if oceans overflow, continents collide, aliens find us,
all jobs disappear and Amazon declares bankruptcy? I try
to watch a movie; they all reinforce my fears.
I find a group of pundits shouting over one another,
jabber indecipherable. Searching for relief, for
entertainment, I encounter dancers. All-but-naked,
gyrating, thrusting dancing partners unable, apparently,
to find a room; comedians who never tasted a bar of soap.
Yearning for the evenings I could watch with my mother,
my kids, I click the remote and there it is: PBS to the
rescue! Pretty girls in pretty dresses with hair-styles
un-reminiscent of basset hounds.

I can understand the words they are singing! I can sway
to familiar melodies! I witness the manners we used to
have! I see respect! Tension drips from my fingertips.
Shoulders un-bunch. My eyes close, pulse slows, heart
opens and my head knows there will be a happy ending.
Thank you, Mr. Welk
for making my Saturday nights great again.

I Walked with a Confident Strut Back Then

through a snazzy restaurant *(upscale* not yet coined)
sleek black dress, heels
filmy turquoise scarf trailing

all eyes on me
it felt like that, anyway
no memory of when

or who I was meeting
I bet he stood up, though
and cheered

That One Evening

My husband didn't mind
and his wife didn't dance
so I slipped into Lionel's arms
and the music took us.
It felt like heaven, gliding,
joyous, each matching movement
a memory-in-the-making.

I don't recall how
we knew them, or her name,
or why we were where we were
wherever that was.
But the passion! Buoyed
in possessive arms,
no will of my own,
each twirl, each step,
each breath, etched.
These many years later I still
thrill to the far-away melody
of a passing train.

Lusting in My Heart Like Jimmy Carter

Averaged out, it's once a decade
but occurred in a fairly, tight bunch
when I was young, of course, with cleavage
sashaying in sky-high heels.

My first boss sent me down the hall on errands
so he could watch me walk
Like Marilyn Monroe he confessed, grinning
He was cute, married, gave me a raise.

Wife by the time I danced with Lionel
our spouses sitting right there. We clung
we swayed, we melted into each other
me thinking, *where else does he move like this?*

The avuncular pharmacist concerned
with the number of pills I was buying
while my husband's job took him far away
offered, over coffee, a cure for loneliness.

Most unforgettable: solo excursion by train
Mate's job far too important to take time off
Stunningly handsome Pullman porter
inviting me to sleep well.

When fellows with flecks of silver in their sideburns
began calling me "Ma'am" I knew my time was up
I culled my wardrobe, discarded the false eyelashes
I'd loved to bat, locked up dear diary once and for all.

Now that I've reached the age of invisibility
(except to actors moonlighting as tip-hungry waiters)
I keep an 8x10 glossy taped inside my nightie drawer
and George Clooney will never know.

Lanais are for Hiding

Years ago, it was my second-cup-of-coffee getaway
while little kids romped inside.
Of course, then we called it screened porch
afterthought on an old farmhouse
built when leisure between labor and bed
was unimaginable.
Mother-ears attuned to bickering, suspect silences,
crocodile tears, I reveled there
in snatches of peace before they found me.

These days, having learned local dialect,
my *lanai* is my martini-with-a-twist getaway.
Chatty neighbor at the front door can't see me.
Solicitors won't know I'm home.
Absent-minded hubby will search out his own glasses.

My hope is, when I reach that Great Lanai in the Sky,
there will be a view. A pillow-y lounge
next to a stack of books. No TV or phones
or breaking news. A soft breeze sighing
through sun-dappled palms.
Maybe, for old time's sake, distant kid-giggles.
Would a bottomless pitcher of Mai Tais be asking too much?

Seminar for Lunch

Newly retired, time on my hands
answered the offer: free lunch
Brawny young fellow came to my house
showed me how bad my water is
"Yuck" he explained. "You drink this?"
He diagnosed, demonstrated, diagrammed
Wow! I could save a bundle on soap
Hour and a half later: a paper to sign
Oh I don't want to buy a water treatment
I just want the free lunch
Geez a big guy can move fast!
almost knocked over the chair
face really red
windows rattled when he slammed the door
He didn't even leave the certificate for lunch
I had to call Home Office three times
before I got it
they said something about flagging my name

Last week I went to one about my bum knee
Sat for evaluation
Doctor must've spent a while
to compile the protocol.
Financial girl explained at length
Insurance would pay three hundred
of the six thousand dollars
Oh, I'm not interested in all that
I can live with this knee
I just heard this was a great place for lunch

Next week I'm lunching
at a place I've never been to before
I signed up to learn about cremation

Best-Laid Plans

My son holds my hand to cross the street,
no longer the little boy I guided.
This is the role reversal I've been dreading.
My gait is slower. He has noticed. Cautiously,
he broaches the subject he's been dreading.

He has attended a seminar, he tells me. At fifty,
he is thinking ahead. Wonders if I am.
You don't know what the future holds. You should have
a plan. "You want an "End of Life Checklist?" I ask.
"You've done your homework. Without my help now."

We smile, remembering. Suddenly, I'm in my mother's house,
a stranger. No right to go through her wallet, search her bureau,
read her letters from John. No right to find hidden bottles of
Henna to keep her hair bright. To wonder why she stored old
powder puffs, why copper pennies littered her cupboards,
why her mink scarf, her wedding ring were missing.

I filled a dumpster with stained dresses, chipped dishes,
greeting cards to Grandma, Aunt, My Dearest, each stack tied
with yellow yarn. I found overdue notices, power shut-off threat,
letters from a law firm. I sat on the floor and wept. Across
from him now, I silently vow, Don't worry, dear son, I will
spare you that. What I would protect you from, if only I could

is the wrenching loss, the pain that goes on and on—
Even knowing, you are punched in the gut.
Joy-filled memories won't save you. Faith won't save you.
It will come with a snippet of song, with the scent
of baking bread, with an unexpected photograph.
Yes, I have a plan. It will save you all but the devastating sorrow.

Underlying It All

I am the music of movies,
the days-gone-by ones, the black and whites.

Silken violins in flickering flames
while lovers whisper; plans are laid.
Frenzied strings for the brandished ax.
I am a 40's dance band behind pretty girls
at the USO. Cheer our boys,
then send them off to hell.
A lilting flute to hurrah the one
who comes marching home.
I'm trombones and French horns and trumpets,
a crescendo of brass to tumble towers,
blaze buildings, chase cars chasing cars,
chasing villains.
Tyrannosaurus Rex rampaging.
I am the drum beat that sways Hawaiian hips.
I am a full orchestra hidden in sagebrush.
Sheriff tracks cowboy tracks Indian.
I am a lone oboe
infiltrating solemn conversations.

How would you know what to feel
if not for me?

photo courtesy of Donna Ward

Peggy Seely is the author of three books of poetry, *Teacups in the Mud*, *Wrestling the Ghosts*, and *Too Many Vases, Not Enough Flowers* (FootHills Publishing). Her poems have appeared in *Connections*, *Packrat*, and *Washout Review*, where she was a contributing editor, as well as several anthologies. She is the winner of several poetry contests including a Slam, has read at Cafe Lena, Saratoga Springs, NY and Florida Porch Cafe, Leesburg, FL in addition to various venues in CT and KY. She has facilitated workshops. She offered poetry as therapy while volunteering at The Bridge Center. Since retiring from a diverse career path, she lives in Florida and enjoys spending summers in the Northeast which she still considers home.

CPSIA information can be obtained
at www.ICGtesting.com
Printed in the USA
BVHW092102011220
594609BV00007B/612

9 781947 653924